D1551332

# just two words
## *for educators*

## karen alonge

*tiny mantras for reaching and teaching*

with deep gratitude
to educators everywhere

in profound recognition of all you do
for our children, our communities,
and our collective future.

# tiny mantras for educators

foster kindness............................................1

never doubt ................................................2

protect dignity ...........................................3

laugh often.................................................4

love learning..............................................5

verify understanding......................................6

not alone ..................................................7

be flexible ................................................8

explain rationale .........................................9

inner voice................................................10

call forth.................................................11

be congruent ..............................................12

apologize first............................................13

carry on...................................................14

come alongside ............................................15

proximity remedy ..........................................16

avoid coercion.............................................17

real world.................................................18

press pause ...............................................19

self care .................................................20

embody integrity ..........................................21

stock snacks ............................................ 22

follow up ................................................. 23

ask politely ............................................. 24

allow exceptions .................................... 25

amplify curiosity ................................... 26

bear witness ............................................ 27

uplifting words ....................................... 28

treasure diversity .................................. 29

what else? ............................................... 30

come closer ............................................. 31

change gears........................................... 32

solicit feedback...................................... 33

future focus............................................. 34

include nature........................................ 35

give space ............................................... 36

tell stories.............................................. 37

look deeper ............................................. 38

given that............................................... 39

collect something.................................. 40

elicit connections.................................. 41

ask permission....................................... 42

you first .................................................. 43

down time .............................................. 44

low voice ................................................ 45

leverage novelty.................................... 46

build bridges ....................................................47

reconsider rewards ...........................................48

what's next? ......................................................49

selective attention ...........................................50

share power .......................................................51

bring yourself ...................................................52

approach gently ...............................................53

trace reactions..................................................54

require sources .................................................55

your thoughts? .................................................56

compare notes...................................................57

what's up? .........................................................58

reading sanctuary ............................................59

think aloud........................................................60

guide transitions .............................................61

lose graciously..................................................62

micro successes..................................................63

I noticed ............................................................64

reliable rhythm ................................................65

exchange expertise...........................................66

be kind................................................................67

dig deep..............................................................68

repair rifts.........................................................69

just one...............................................................70

calibrate assistance..........................................71

transparent effort................................... 72

nurture teamwork.................................. 73

permit doodling..................................... 74

thank you.............................................. 75

supportive structure.............................. 76

keep going ............................................ 77

think twice ........................................... 78

calming zone......................................... 79

brainstorm solutions ............................ 80

watchful waiting.................................... 81

benign hypothesis................................. 82

break habits.......................................... 83

back off ................................................ 84

regulate together .................................. 85

go home ............................................... 86

forget fairness....................................... 87

switch seats .......................................... 88

maintain equanimity.............................. 89

sherlock holmes .................................... 90

inner drive ............................................ 91

rehearse strategies ............................... 92

contribute together................................ 93

calm clarity .......................................... 94

seek positives........................................ 95

emotional tolerance............................... 96

keep learning............................................97

venting partner ........................................98

express concerns ......................................99

civil conversation ................................. 100

what matters........................................... 101

write notes.............................................. 102

* using this book for professional development
............................................................ 103

# foster kindness

when class morale feels low,
get energy flowing again
by inviting your students
to write notes of appreciation
to other people in the school:
the janitor, the bus driver,
other teachers, and support staff.

help students deliver the notes
in person, so they can witness
the impact of genuine gratitude
on both the receiver
and the giver.

# never doubt

that you are making a difference.

your kindness, encouragement, and respect
create a permanent imprint on your
students' hearts and minds.

as they grow up and go about their lives,
they will deliver your influence
far and wide,
to people and places
you will never see.

# protect dignity

whenever possible,
offer your feedback, corrections
and suggestions
in private.

public humiliation
rarely calls forth
the best in anyone.

# laugh often

at yourself, especially.

light and playful laughter after a blunder
demonstrates that your ego does not need
to defend itself against being wrong.

your humility and self-acceptance
will set a powerful example
that may someday equip a student
to walk away
instead of fight.

# love learning

your attitude toward learning
is contagious.

your own joy and enthusiasm
for reading, researching
and discussing new ideas
may well be
the most impactful and enduring gift
you can give to your students.

# verify understanding

just because you said it clearly
does not mean it was understood.

ask students to summarize their learning.

even better,
ask them what they are taking away
from the lesson
that will be *useful* for them.

# not alone

you see and feel
so much every day,
and far too much of it
is heartbreaking.

too many students
show up at school
with empty stomachs
and wounded psyches.

yet you try,
again and again,
to equip them with the tools they'll need
to build a better life someday.

it's absolutely essential
to have someone in your world
who can simply listen with compassion
while you unburden your heart,
so you can go back the next day,
and do it all again.

p.s. *thank you*

# be flexible

adapting your plan
in response to new information
is not a sign of weakness.

instead, flexibility is evidence
of awareness, strength, and wisdom.

# explain rationale

when you communicate
your requirements or requests,
take the time to explain your reasoning.

even if kids don't like or agree
with your rationale,
since they feel included and respected,
they are less likely to interpret your policies
as a personal challenge to their autonomy
that must be met with resistance.

# inner voice

when you address a student directly,
choose your words very carefully.

because you are in a position
of respected authority,
they may absorb your perspective
as the unquestionable truth.

if you knew
that what you are about to say
would be repeated incessantly
by this young person's inner voice
for years, decades, or a lifetime,
would you still say it?

# call forth

give students the benefit of the doubt,
and you may be surprised
by how earnestly
they will strive
to be worthy of it.

# be congruent

students pay more attention
to what you do,
and how you do it,
than to what you say.

they will be neither fooled
nor impressed
by hypocrisy.

for maximum impact,
your words and your actions
must match.

# apologize first

missteps are inevitable.
you are only human, after all!
but even your mistakes
can become a learning opportunity
for your students.

begin with *I'm sorry*
but don't stop there.

also offer to
repair any harm
that resulted
from your actions.

# carry on

a great deal of your work
involves sowing strong and healthy seeds
in the fertile young minds
that look to you for guidance.

much will need to happen underground
before those seeds can sprout.

don't let the delay discourage you.
just keep planting.

# come alongside

when you find yourself in
a power struggle
that feels like a tug-of-war,
drop the rope.

call a time-out
so you can try to see the situation
from your student's perspective.

there's a reason they are resisting.

shifting your position
to one of respectful curiosity
can help you find out
what that reason is.

without that information,
resolution without resentment
is quite a longshot.

# proximity remedy

your physical presence
and calm demeanor
are interventions
in and of themselves.

when you notice a student
starting to get off track,
ask them to help you
with a simple task
that requires them to
come closer to you.

*Will you help me straighten this rug?*
*I could use an extra hand with these papers.*
*Would you mind helping me erase the board?*

Just being near you,
even without talking about the issue at all,
jump-starts emotional regulation.

# avoid coercion

instead of using force, guilt, bribes, threats,
punishment, or consequences,
help students to recognize their options.

only then will they be in the position
to make an informed choice
about which course of action is most likely
to take them where they want to go.

# real world

we learn best
in context.

how will learning
what you are teaching
help your students
achieve something they want?

money management,
sport statistics,
construction, cooking,
music ...
there are so many
real world applications
that they already care about.

and if you are not sure what
they find interesting, ask!

relevance is a shortcut to learning integration.

# press pause

a sense of urgency
is often the enemy
of creativity.

are you absolutely certain
that this problem you are facing
requires an immediate solution?

# self care

when your own vessel
runs dry
you have nothing of value
to serve to others.

prioritize activities
and relationships
that fill you up
with love, energy,
and joy.

# embody integrity

do what you say you will.
keep your word.
follow through.

and when you can't,
which will inevitably happen at some point,
own up to it,
in advance if possible.

take responsibility by
communicating the delay/issue,
and re-negotiating a new plan.

# stock snacks

sadly, too many students
come to school hungry.

and even if kids have eaten,
certain types of trauma history
can lead to food insecurity,
where children live in constant fear
that there will not be enough
for them to eat.

ask helpful parents to
keep your room stocked
with fruit and granola bars.

when students know that "brain food"
is always available to them,
no questions asked,
you can all turn your attention
back to the business of
teaching and learning.

# follow up

whenever there's an incident,
circle back later to see
how they are processing it.

find out what they need
in order to fully integrate
what they learned
from the experience,
so everyone can move on.

# ask politely

students,
parents,
colleagues,
and administrators
rarely respond favorably
to demands.

# allow exceptions

but teach them how
to appropriately ask for one:
by making a proposal
that includes
their reasons for asking,
what they *are* able to do,
a reasonable timeline,
and a plan to mitigate the impact
their exception would have on others,
including you.

if you are satisfied with their proposal,
grant it.

if you are not, invite them to make adjustments
and re-submit it to you.

# amplify curiosity

it's energizing and mobilizing
for students to hear you say
*Gosh, what a great question!*
*I'm not sure what the answer is.*
*How can we find out?*

# bear witness

sometimes there is simply no way
to alleviate another's suffering.

bearing witness
means not looking away
to avoid the pain
of observing
that which we cannot change.

you may feel as though
your presence and warm attention
are deeply insufficient.

but to your student,
it could make all the difference
simply to have a compassionate
and non-judgmental observer
keeping them company.

# uplifting words

they probably already receive
plenty of criticism
elsewhere.

# treasure diversity

welcome and celebrate
the variety of opinions,
preferences,
and learning styles
in your classroom.

individual differences
strengthen the whole.

# what else?

while listening to an upset student,
summarize what you've heard them say
and then ask
*what else?*

continue summarizing and eliciting
until they have nothing left to add.

only then will the student be ready
to answer questions like
*what do you need?*
and
*how can I help?*

# come closer

if you hear yourself thinking
*she's only doing that for attention,*
perhaps it would be beneficial
to offer your attention
preventatively.

attention is a fundamental human need,
not a pathological one.

it cannot be punished,
consequenced, reasoned,
or ignored away.

when the need for attention is met,
attention-seeking behaviors
usually quiet down
on their own.

# change gears

if something
isn't going over well,
set it aside
and do something else.

conditions may be
more conducive to success
another time.

# solicit feedback

every so often, ask students
what they want you to
stop doing,
keep doing,
and start doing.

providing clear and helpful feedback
is a very important life skill.

and so is receiving it gracefully.

# future focus

so they made an attempt,
and it didn't work out as they'd hoped.

it's not a failure if they learned something!

ask what they know now
that they didn't know before they tried,
and how they can incorporate
that new information
into a revised strategy
for next time.

# include nature

bring in rocks and sticks and bugs.
raise a class pet,
or even just a class plant.

any living thing
can serve as a reminder
for students of all ages
that there are natural rhythms
and cycles,
and things are not always
as they seem.

it also gives students
something to nurture.
learning how to help
another living thing thrive
is quite an empowering experience.

# give space

when resistance arises,
step back.

don't pressure
or plead
or attempt to convince.

respect their autonomy.
emphasize it, even.

given time and space,
they will often choose
to come around
on their own.

# tell stories

warm ones, please.
about people being kind, generous,
and helpful.

kids see and hear far too much bad news.

violent words and images
that are casually consumed and discarded
by adults around them
take root in their tender psyches,
terrifying them to the core.

bring balance
to their perception of the world
by sharing stories
about the best of humanity.

# look deeper

when kids are acting out at school,
it can be very illuminating
to consider what is going on
in their lives outside of school.

trauma-informed educators
do not ask
*what is wrong with that student?*

instead they wonder
*what happened (or is happening) to that student?*
and
*what is strong in that student?*

# given that

sometimes students make
outlandish and unreasonable requests,
like:
*Won't you just give me credit anyway?*
*Can't you just say I was here?*
*Just give me one more day!?*

you can rein that in a bit
by naming the boundaries
of the playing field:
*Given that we have to follow school rules,*
or
*Given that I have a deadline I need to meet,*
or
*Given that none of us can change the law,*

followed by:
*What could we/you do?*

# collect something

purple elephants,
rocks,
the swag of a favorite team.

it's not important what it is.

what's important
is that when your students,
in a moment of open-hearted generosity,
want to make or draw
something for you,
they can feel confident
in advance
that you will like it.

# elicit connections

what does what they just learned
remind them of?

how might it be useful in
resolving a seemingly non-related
issue or problem?

weaving a web of connections
and relevance
makes recall much easier.

# ask permission

when you ask if they
are interested in hearing
your thoughts,
or whether now is a good
time to discuss this further,
you are demonstrating respect
and modeling requesting consent.

you are also inviting them
to mentally clear some room
to consider your perspective.

# you first

before you ask or tell a student
to calm down,
make sure to calm yourself.

their nervous systems
are wired for imitation
and entrainment.

it really speeds up the process
if you can lead the way.

and when you can't calm yourself,
let that be a helpful reminder
of just how challenging it truly is
for their immature
and inexperienced brains
to compose themselves
on command.

# down time

whenever possible,
structure your students' days
with a tiny break between activities.

even if it's just one full breath
and a standing stretch.

resting and recharging are
just as important for productivity
as working.

# low voice

have you noticed how quickly
kids become immune
to yelling?

# leverage novelty

sing it.
drum it.
paint it.
dance it.
act it out.

make content fun, silly or weird
and it will be more likely to stick.

# build bridges

even your most incorrigible student
loves someone, something,
or some place.

we are more alike than different
at the core.

common ground
may not be
very far away.

# reconsider rewards

rewards are risky.

when students believe
that whatever it takes to earn a reward
is beyond their capacity, they may
give up or act like they don't care.

do you want your students
performing for rewards
or making the decision
to behave in a certain way
because it makes sense to them
and helps them meet their goals?

a quiet word from you
acknowledging effort, intention,
or restraint
often goes much further
than a gold star.

# what's next?

to help teach consequential thinking,
create as many practice opportunities
as you possibly can.

*What might happen next?*
*What could we do next?*
*What might be the outcome*
*of each of these choices?*

don't be telling
when you could be asking.

# selective attention

wanted or unwanted,
the behaviors and attitudes
you feed with your attention
will flourish.

choose your focus wisely.

# share power

you don't have to solve every
behavioral issue in the classroom
on your own.

in fact, it's often more productive
to work together with your students
to identify the unsolved problems
and generate potential solutions.

make sure to come back together
after experimenting with solutions
to determine whether they work
or need revising in order to be effective.

# bring yourself

love scuba, giraffes, or Haiti?

your quirky areas of interest
make you unique and real
to your students.

let your passion be visible
in your classroom.

show delight
when your students surprise you
with new and interesting facts about it.

kids always benefit
from witnessing an adult
who is curious and engaged.

# approach gently

when you need to intervene
or redirect,
walk lightly and speak softly.

approach slowly from the front,
rather than taking them by surprise
from the side or the back.

confrontational words,
body language,
or tone of voice
usually trigger defensiveness,
not thoughtful behavior adjustments.

# trace reactions

your response is never determined
by what they said or did,
but only by your beliefs and assumptions.

assume they meant harm,
and you'll respond with anger.

assume they were fearful,
and you are more likely
to respond with compassion.

if you want to change your default reactions,
question the stories you tell yourself
about the meaning behind their actions.

# require sources

even in the early elementary years,
whenever a student shares a fact with you,
cheerfully ask them to identify their source.

if they don't know
or can't remember,
help them find it.

then assess it together
for bias, reliability,
and statistical accuracy.

much damage has been done
in our society
by unsubstantiated claims.

creating a classroom culture
of verification
contributes to a well-informed
and media literate
citizenship.

# your thoughts?

whenever you teach a new skill or concept,
ask the students what they think about it.

in order to generate and share their opinions,
they first need to absorb the material.

sneaky, eh?

# compare notes

stuck? bored? worried?

discuss your problems
and concerns
with your colleagues.

they are a local and dependable
resource for feedback, suggestions,
and creative brainstorming.

as an added bonus,
helping you may distract them
from their own problems,
or jump start
their own solutions.

# what's up?

students do what they do
for reasons that makes sense to them.

sometimes it's because they don't
have the ability or capacity
to do anything else in that moment.

sometimes they simply act from habit
without stopping to consider alternatives.

naming what you've observed
in non-judgmental language:
*I see you away from your desk,*
then asking W*hat's up?*
not only allows them
to take a look at what's
going on for them,
but their reply also cues you in
to any deficits, barriers or issues
you can help them address.

# reading sanctuary

create a cozy spot
where your students
can lose themselves
in a book.

the day-to-day experiences
of too many kids
are utterly devastating.

make it easy for them
to escape for a while.

# think aloud

narrate your thought process
while trouble-shooting.

witnessing a calm and regulated adult
generating a solution
helps kids understand
and acquire the skill.

*Gosh, it's hot in here,*
*and these windows don't open.*
*Maybe I can wheel the white board*
*in front of the window*
*to block out the sun.*

*Oh, I see it's not tall enough.*
*I wonder what else I could try?*

# guide transitions

don't view class transitions
as your time to do other things.

lots of undesirable behavior,
including bullying,
can occur during the unstructured shift
from one activity to another.

staying close and engaged
and offering your warm attention
will help everyone feel
supported and safe.

consequently, they will settle
more efficiently
into the next activity.

and then you can do other things.

# lose graciously

good sportsmanship is
a very useful life skill,
and students may not
see it modeled
at home or on TV.

let them watch you
take losing in stride
by congratulating the winner,
and thanking them for
the good game.

# micro successes

what you may not realize
as you scold him
for forgetting his book
is what a heroic effort it took
for him to make it to class
at all.

perhaps he only invested that energy
because he feels safe with you.

please don't take that for granted.

# I noticed

a neutral, non-judgmental observation
is a very effective on-ramp
to collaboration and cooperation.

just state the facts:
*I notice coats and mittens on the floor.*
*I see that the door is open.*
*Looks like the hamster's water bottle is empty.*

giving students a chance to act
in response to impersonal information
can avert the compulsion
to defend themselves
against feeling shamed or blamed.

# reliable rhythm

create a consistent flow
to the days and weeks;
an orderly progression
of activities,
with embedded cues
about upcoming transitions.

students are comforted
by knowing what to expect.

predictability
creates a sense of safety.

# exchange expertise

of course you are
a subject matter expert,
but there's one topic
that your students will always
know more about than you do:
their own experience.

Only they know
what life feels like
from inside their skin.

If we are respectful,
open-minded,
and non-judgmental,
they may teach us
what we need to know
to be able to teach them.

# be kind

many of your students
and colleagues
are struggling mightily
with hidden challenges.

if you were able to see and understand
what they are going through,
your judgment
would effortlessly melt
into compassion.

# dig deep

become a seeker of strengths.
every student has them.

the harder they are to discover,
the more crucial it is
that you succeed in your search.

# repair rifts

we all have times
when we are on our last nerve
and say something we regret.

as soon as we return to ourselves again,
it's essential to acknowledge
the harm we caused,
sincerely apologize,
and offer to repair it.

kids learn relationship maintenance
by witnessing adults
humbly and sincerely
taking responsibility
for their actions.

# just one

researchers tell us
that just one adult
who sees and accepts
a child's whole self,
including their good intentions,
their desire to help rather than hurt,
and their need for creativity and connection,
is enough to foster
resilience and self-respect
in that child.

and no pressure,
but that adult
could be you.

# calibrate assistance

help students who ask,
but only just until
they can help themselves.

eroding their dignity,
self-respect,
or confidence
is not helpful.

# transparent effort

let kids see you
refusing to give up.

if you don't succeed
in your initial attempt,
make an adjustment
to your strategy
and try again.

repeat until it works.

they'll remember
and emulate
your persistence.

# nurture teamwork

tossing students together
into a group project
without providing significant
structure, support, and oversight
rarely fosters real teamwork.

it's much more likely to breed
resentment, freeloading, and
an uneven distribution
of the workload to those
who are most conscientious.

think carefully about what you
want students to learn about
collaboration and participation.

then make sure your supervision,
feedback, and grading strategy
support your goal.

# permit doodling

or coloring pages,
or small, silent fidget toys,
as long as they don't disturb others,
and still get their work done.

some students find it
much easier to pay attention
when their hands are engaged.

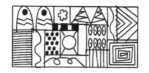

# thank you

maybe it was their job to do it,
or they had promised,
or you assigned the task to them.

thank them anyway.

no one enjoys
being taken for granted.

# supportive structure

sometimes what looks
like procrastination
or a lack of motivation
is actually
a genuine inability
to plan or prioritize.

some students need help
breaking large tasks
into small steps,
fitting them into a timeline,
and troubleshooting potential obstacles.

a bit of supportive structure
co-created with you up front,
will help them eventually learn
how to generate their own.

# keep going

you are creating a ripple effect
as you pass through students' lives,
but you won't be able to tell.

if you pause and turn around to look for it,
you'll stop creating it,
and it might look like
you are not making any difference
at all.

so don't stop to look for evidence.
just keep forging ahead.

* inspired by ZM

# think twice

before you take action,
identify exactly what
you wish to accomplish.

then ask yourself:
*is this truly the best way?*

# calming zone

create a space in your classroom
that supports self-regulation,
even if it's only a beanbag chair
that faces the window.
(or even better, a fish tank!)

designating a calming spot
empowers students to take a break
when they need to, which fosters
self-awareness and self-regulation.

it also provides the other students
with a clear "do not disturb" signal.

# brainstorm solutions

when you encounter a
dynamic, situation, or group behavior
that needs to stop,
call a class meeting and
explain the situation
as objectively as possible.

asking your students
what they think would work
seamlessly transforms them
into part of the solution.

# watchful waiting

some conflicts
work themselves out
eventually.

in the meantime,
keep a close eye
on the situation
to ensure
everyone's safety.

# benign hypothesis

if you are unable
to directly confirm
a student's intention,
treat her as if
she meant well
and needs adult assistance
to figure out a more
effective strategy.

# break habits

not everything in your routine
is serving you.

stir things up periodically.
see what rises to the surface
and wants to evaporate away.

# back off

when you become angry or upset,
politely but quickly disengage
and calm yourself down.

while you take your break,
the other party also
receives an opportunity
to compose themselves.

# regulate together

many students have never really learned
how to calm themselves down.

so when you send them away,
to the principal's office, the hall,
or even to a corner of the room,
rather than calming down, they may escalate.
fear, shame, embarrassment and disconnection
are incompatible with calm composure.

instead, if you need to curtail disruption in class,
escort them to a calm adult
who knows how to foster co-regulation,
and will engage with them while walking,
making music, playing a game,
or creating art together.

kids learn how to self-regulate
by interacting with
self-regulating adults.
make sure you have some available.

# go home

sometimes you just need
to get out of there
because nothing productive
is resulting from further
effort or conversation.

go home.
enjoy a nourishing meal,
and a good night's rest.

you can try again tomorrow.

# forget fairness

rather than striving to meet
the impossible goal of
treating every student exactly the same,
explain that you will try to
assess and meet their individual needs,
which will look different for each of them.

this will put a quick end
to the need for scorekeeping.

# switch seats

periodically take a look
at yourself, your classroom,
and your instruction
through the eyes of your students.
you might even literally
sit in one of their chairs.

then make adjustments
accordingly.

# maintain equanimity

it's possible to become almost impervious
to emotional contagion.

just because they are upset,
does not mean you need to be.

learn to stay centered in your own experience
rather than being battered about
by the fluctuating emotional weather
around you.

# sherlock holmes

become a detective
searching for clues about what is
interfering with each student's
ability to activate their full potential.

are they hungry? not getting enough sleep?
in physical or emotional pain?
having trouble with visual tracking?

if you simply assume
they are "difficult"
you risk overlooking
any removable barriers
in their inner or outer
environment.

# inner drive

over-reliance on extrinsic rewards
is toxic to intrinsic motivation.

most students find
an internal experience of
autonomy, mastery,
and purpose
far more gratifying
than praise or prizes.

# rehearse strategies

it's not enough for students
to simply hear or read
about social and emotional skills
like anger management,
conflict resolution,
or self-regulation.

they need to try them,
over and over again,
in a variety of settings and scenarios.

provide opportunities
for them to practice these skills
every single day.

# contribute together

find a way
for your class to join together
in making a meaningful contribution
to the community.

planting flowers,
chalking sidewalk murals,
picking up trash,
or feeding the hungry
help kids feel like
genuine members of society
who can make a real difference.

# calm clarity

kids feel safer
when they know
exactly what is expected of them.

if we keep moving the boundaries
without explaining why we've
changed our rules
or made an exception today,
it's disconcerting for them.
they prefer predictability
to randomness.

they are reassured by
your warm, kind clarity
even when they don't appreciate
the limits you have set.

# seek positives

acknowledge effort and intention
not simply outcome.

be someone
who builds students up
rather than
cutting them down.

forget about giving constructive criticism.
there is no such thing.

# emotional tolerance

learn to accept
your students' feelings of displeasure
and disapproval.

it's ok if they are not happy
about your policies, rules or expectations.
they don't necessarily need to like it
in order to go along with it.

let them express their disagreement,
with respect and civility, of course.
summarize their position or perspective
to demonstrate that you are actively listening.

once they feel their protest has been truly *heard*,
many kids find it easier
to let it go.

but if we tell them
their feelings are unfounded
or try to convince them "this will be fun!"
they often become more agitated.

# keep learning

work with an instructional coach.
seek out cutting edge professional development.
test out new approaches and ask for feedback.
take learning risks, make mistakes,
and process them out loud with your students.

it's good for them to understand
that you are a student, too.

# venting partner

kids can sense our hostility and resentment
even when we think we are hiding it well.

locate a friend or colleague
who can listen without judgment
to your anger, frustration and fears
so these emotions don't leak out
onto your students.

your feelings are valid,
albeit usually temporary,
and you deserve to be heard.

venting is a lot like taking out the garbage.
it restores inner harmony and order,
so we can think clearly again.

be sure to return the favor when you can.

# express concerns

concerns are not criticisms.
they provide information.

*I'm concerned that the handle might break.*
*I'm concerned that it will be impossible to catch up.*
*I'm concerned that someone might trip on it.*

you can follow up with a request if you'd like:
*Please set that down on the ground now.*
*Let's see if we can come up with an alternative.*
*I'd like you to hang that on the hook, please.*

communicating your concerns
expands their critical thinking skills,
and makes it evident that you are not
just trying to control their behavior
in order to disempower them.

# civil conversation

class discussion topic:
how can we
stay respectful of each other
when our opinions and
interpretations differ?

and how will we feel
about ourselves
and each other
when we succeed at doing so?

# what matters

challenge yourself
to discover
just one thing
that is important
to each of your students.

# write notes

catch students being good citizens,
going the extra mile,
or striving for excellence,
and write a little note
of affirmation and validation.

leave it where they can find it,
or hand it to them in private
without fanfare.

decades later,
many of them
will still have that note
in their possession.

*that*
is how important
you truly are.

# * using this book for professional development

This book is about the power of *being*. Educators wield tremendous influence as they interact, communicate, and accomplish everyday tasks in front of their students. Each of you has been gifted with the opportunity and authority to teach by example the most important lesson your students will ever learn: *how to be a kind, responsible and decent person.*

Below are a few suggestions for facilitated exercises in case you'd like to integrate this book into professional development sessions.

Exploratory questions:
a) *Summarize the main concept on this page.*
b) *Discuss someone you know who embodies this quality/concept, and how you feel about yourself when you're with them.*
c) *How might applying this concept make a difference for you/us? For our students?*
d) *What steps could we take to activate and integrate this concept into our work?*

1) Facilitator opens book at random and reads one page to the room. Small breakout groups discuss the exploratory questions related to that page. After the discussions conclude, allow time for participants to jot down "notes to self" about their takeaways.

2) Pair off. Each pair opens the book at random and discusses the exploratory questions about the page they've selected. All pairs then rejoin the larger group. Each pair reads their page out loud, then reports the answers they generated and facilitates any ensuing discussion. End with time for notes to self.

3) Individuals open their book at random and journal using the exploratory questions. They then form groups of three and share what they've written with each other. After each person shares, they shift into observer mode and listen silently while the other two have a conversation about what they just said. It's ok for the observer to jot down notes, but not to speak or participate in their conversation in any way. When the pair discussion finishes, the observer reports to the other two any insights they gained while listening. Continue until all three have been observers.

to contact karen
or learn more about
her work, please visit

**www.karenalonge.com**


to contact marc
or learn more about
his design work,
please visit

**www.marc-hudson.com**